Words for every prayer occasion - at your fingertips

Introducing THE IDEALS TREASURY OF PRAYER

In this beautifully illustrated book you'll find the words for every prayer occasion at your fingertips. Here are prayers of praise, for healing, for comfort, for joy, for forgiveness, for strength, for guidance . . . each placed into the appropriate chapter. These prayers will inspire and help you make all your "wants and wishes known."

You'll find prayers for strength and for courage, such as a lovely poetic prayer by Amy Carmichel . . . you'll find prayers seeking forgiveness, such as one by Peter Marshall, who used everyday language so eloquently . . . and you'll find prayers asking for wisdom such as one by John Calvin . . . and prayers for compassion by William Barcla.

160 pages, full color throughout, heavy weight enamel stock, deluxe hard cover binding.

But there's even more included than wonderful prayer, you'll find Scripture verses and quotations that will inspire you in your daily quiet time. And you'll appreciate Christian testimonial explaining how others have found richer, and more rewarding lives.

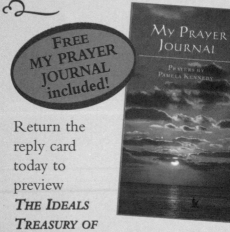

FREE MY PRAYER JOURNAL included!

Return the reply card today to preview THE IDEALS TREASURY OF PRAYER for 21 days FREE. . . . and receive a FREE *My Prayer Journal*.

NO NEED TO SEND MONEY NOW!

COMPLETE CARD AND MAIL TODAY FOR 21 DAYS FREE EXAMINATION.

FREE EXAMINATION CERTIFICATE

YES! I'd like to examine *THE IDEALS TREASURY OF PRAYER* for 21 days FREE. If after 21 days I am not delighted with it, I may return it and owe nothing. If I decide to keep it, I will be billed $24.95, plus shipping and processing. In either case, the FREE My Prayer Journal is mine to keep.

Total copies ordered _____

Please print your name and address:

_____
NAME

_____
ADDRESS   APT#

_____
CITY   STATE   ZIP

Allow 4 weeks for delivery. Orders subject to credit approval.
Send no money now. We will bill you later.
www.IdealsBooks.com   15/202329239

P9-BBM-831

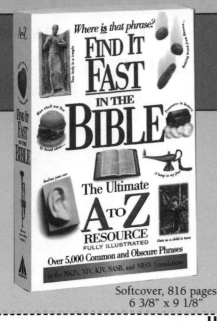

Softcover, 816 pages
6 3/8" x 9 1/8"

Find Buried Treasures in Your Bible
Find the Verses You Want—
at Your Fingertips!

Sometimes looking for a Bible verse is like looking for a needle in a haystack. But now you can head straight to the passage you want with the help of a new kind of Bible aid: *Find it Fast in the Bible* lets you look up a fragment of a phrase instead of an individual word and takes you directly to the exact chapter and verse.

Now it's easy to find what you're searching for in the Bible—without relying on your memory! *Find it Fast in the Bible* works like a concordance, but with an advantage. *Find it Fast in the Bible* is just right for anyone who wants to know the Bible better—and find what they're looking for in a flash. It's perfect for Bible veterans and new-comers alike. It also makes a great gift for family and friends—it's a gift that keeps on giving!

FIND IT FAST IN THE BIBLE
Gives you a shortcut to the answers you're seeking!

✔ Easier to use than a concordance

✔ Look up phrases instead of individual words

✔ Keyed to all major translations

✔ Over 800 pages with over 5,000 best-loved and most-used phrases

✔ More than 30,000 references

FREE EXAMINATION CERTIFICATE

YES! I'd like to examine *Find it Fast in the Bible*, at no risk or obligation. If I decide to keep the book, I will be billed later at the low Guideposts price of only $13.95, plus shipping and processing. If not completely satisfied, I may return the book within 30 days and owe nothing. The FREE *Magnet Picture Frame* is mine to keep no matter what I decide.

Total copies ordered: _____

Please print your name and address:

_____
NAME

_____
ADDRESS   APT#

_____
CITY   STATE   ZIP

Allow 4 weeks for delivery. Orders subject to credit approval.
Send no money now. We will bill you later.
www.guideposts.org

Printed in USA
11/202329241

We'll send you this colorful Magnet Picture Frame **FREE** when you say "YES!" to our 30-day Free Preview Offer. This 2-in-1 magnet pulls apart to form a picture frame —perfect for photos of friends and loved ones—plus, a passage from Scripture to brighten your day!

Yes, I have loved you with an everlasting love...
Jer 31:3

FREE
2-IN-1 MAGNET

ideals®
COUNTRY

2005

Dedicated to a celebration of the American ideals of faith in God, loyalty to country, and love of family.

Features

Departments

Cover: Purple coneflowers and black-eyed Susans share the spotlight in a garden near Vashon Island, Washington. Photograph by Terry Donnelly/Donnelly Austin Photography.

Inside front and back covers: This mountain hideaway in Diane Phelan's painting entitled SISTERS SAMPLER *invites observers to envision themselves spending the summer day relaxing beside the stream and watching the clouds drift among the mountain peaks. Painting © Diane Phelan Watercolors. All rights reserved.*

IDEALS—Vol. 62, No. 3 June 2005 IDEALS (ISSN 0019-137X, USPS 256-240) is published six times a year: January, March, May, July, September, and November by Ideals Publications, a division of Guideposts, 39 Seminary Hill Road, Carmel, NY 10512. Copyright © 2005 by Ideals Publications, a division of Guideposts. All rights reserved. The cover and entire contents of IDEALS are fully protected by copyright and must not be reproduced in any manner whatsoever. Title IDEALS registered U.S. Patent Office. Printed and bound in USA. Printed on Weyerhaeuser Husky. The paper used in this publication meets the minimum requirements of American National Standard for Information Sciences—Permanence of Paper for Printed Library Materials, ANSI Z39.48-1984. Periodicals postage paid at Carmel, New York, and additional mailing offices. Canadian mailed under Publications Mail Agreement Number 40010140. POSTMASTER: Send address changes to IDEALS, 39 Seminary Hill Road, Carmel, NY 10512. CANADA POST: Send address changes to Guideposts PO Box 1051, Fort Erie ON L2A 6C7. For subscription or customer service questions, contact Ideals Publications, a division of Guideposts, 39 Seminary Hill Road, Carmel, NY 10512. Fax 845-228-2115. Reader Preference Service: We occasionally make our mailing lists available to other companies whose products or services might interest you. If you prefer not to be included, please write to Ideals Customer Service.

ISBN 0-8249-1302-7   GST 893989236

For subscription information and submission guidelines, visit www.idealsbooks.com

COUNTRY BORN

Eiluned Lewis

We who were born   The pike and the salmon,
In country places   The bull and the horse,
Far from cities   The curlew's cry
And shifting faces,   And the smell of gorse.
We have a birthright   Pride of trees,
No man can sell   Swiftness of streams,
And a secret joy   Magic of frost
No man can tell.   Have shaped our dreams.
For we are kindred   No baser vision
To lordly things: Their spirit fills
The wild duck's flight   Who walk by right
And the white owl's wings, On the naked hills.

SUMMER PASTORALE

May Allread Baker

Give me a catbird in a tree
Showering the air with melody;
A flock of geese; a hissing gander
Near where willowed streams meander;
Droning bees in fields of clover;
Fragrant breezes whispering over.
Give me a faithful canine friend,
An ally till my journey's end;
The sight of placid, large-eyed cows
And upland pastures where they browse.
Far from the city's noise and strife,
Give me the simple country life.

*A red barn is framed by lupines on a farm near Franconia,
New Hamsphire. Photograph by William H. Johnson.*

3

Summer Magic
Doris Gregerson

The river wends its restless way
Through clear, cool eve of summer day.
Cottonwoods shed their downy charms
While bullfrogs croak throaty alarms.
The robins sing in poplar trees;
Their voices blend with bumblebees'
And chirping crickets', loud and shrill.
Wonderland beckons, and I thrill
To endless pleasure—sight and sound—
And summer's magic treasures found.

A Quiet Place
D. A. Hoover

Beneath white limestone cliffs,
Our spring sent crystal waters running
Along a golden gravel path
With lazy turtles sunning.
When summer days were close and hot,
We gathered new-mown hay;
And in the languid afternoon,
We often slipped away
To sip cold water and relax
With summer's drowsy mood
And rest beneath tall sycamores
In shady solitude.

Things I Love
Daisy Covin Walker

I love to sit by a shallow stream
And watch the water ripple
     over small pebbles
And there weave my long daydream,
Away from the world's worry and troubles.
I love to lie beneath a leafy tree
And look up high at the blue sky,
See the leaves create a fancy pattern of lace
While sail-clouds like a flimsy veil flit by.
I love a clouded sunset
With the sun gently peeping through
Cloud-castles tinted from fawn
     to rosy hues.
I love a slow, drowsy dawn;
The beautiful awakening of day;
The twittering of birds on my lawn;
The mysterious night slipping away.
I love to stand on a high hill,
Scan the deep emerald valleys below,
See the friendly, peaceful rill
Like a silver ribbon zigzagging its flow.
I love the twilight shadows,
Silhouetted trees against the sky,
The vast sweet silence
Of day's gentle passing by.

Peaks of the Sawtooth Range stand guard over a grassy meadow in the Sawtooth Natural Recreation Area in Idaho. Photograph by Mary Liz Austin/Donnelly Austin Photography.

Give Me a Day

O. J. Robertson

Give me a day when winds blow free
And white clouds scurry over;
I'll lock my door and hurry forth
And be a gypsy rover.
I'll journey to the splashing sea
Where the waves swell wild and wide;
I'll wash my face in the salty spray
Of the savage, surging tide.
I'll visit neighbors of the wood,
Great oak and towering pine;
Inherit a hundred years of peace
From those ancient friends of mine.
Give me a day when wild winds sweep
Over hill slopes green and high;
I'll race to the summit's tallest peak
Flinging kisses to the sky.

*Waves gallantly attempt to surge up the sides of
sandstone cliffs at Cape Kiwanda near Tillamook
County, Oregon. Photograph by Steve Terrill.*

Beauty of Our Land

Bessie Trull Law

Oftentimes our dreams are forming
Where the winds and waters sing;
Where the rugged trails are winding
Through a meadow to a spring
Rushing from a snow-capped mountain;
Warbling with a passing breeze;
Rippling rhythms toward a fountain
Framed in swaying willow trees;

Far from all the crash and rumble
Of a busy city street.
With our spirits high, but humble,
While we stroll at Nature's feet,
Let her music charm and cheer us
Till the heart can understand
That a Father's love is near us
In the beauty of the land.

The Gold of Summer

Wilfred E. Beaver

Long bars of golden light slant down
Through the oak tree's canopy;
And, shadow-flecked, the hillside lies
Near the brook's soft melody.

The drowsy bees go humming by
Like treasure ships of lore
That, steering through an unknown sea,
Find wealth along the shore.

Like gold, the fragrant hay is piled
In heaps beneath the trees,
And summer dreams are wafting by
On each caressing breeze.

Brilliant poppies cover the hillsides near Antelope Valley, California. Photograph by Carr Clifton.

Golden Days
Margaret Williams Stevens

Here's to the blue-gold days of summer,
Far skyline and field of wheat,
Old road curving past a meadow,
Cool grass underneath my feet,
Cloud-boats dipping, drifting closer,
Catfish tugging on my line—
Everything seems close to heaven
In the peaceful summertime.

June
Catherine Eckrich

To look across the wheat field's tossing sea
Splashing against a shining rim of sky;
To hear a slow and sibilant tune
Whispering through the dancing spears;
To lie immersed within the ocean of the afternoon
Feeling the green and golden waves slide by;
Sometimes I think that this is heaven enough,
Heaven enough, this singing sea and I afloat
These fragrant waves of June.

The Summer Pool
Cosmo Monkhouse

There is a singing in the summer air,
The blue and brown moths flutter o'er the grass,
The stubble bird is creaking in the wheat,
And perch'd upon the honeysuckle-hedge
Pipes the green linnet. Oh, the golden world!
The stir of life on every blade of grass,
The motion and the joy on every bough,
The glad feast everywhere, for things that love
The sunshine, and for things that love the shade!

If We Knew
May Riley Smith

Let us gather up the sunbeams
     Lying all around our path;
Let us keep the wheat and roses,
     Casting out the thorns and chaff;
Let us find our sweetest comfort
     In the blessings of today,
With a patient hand removing
     All the briars from the way.

A field of golden wheat in St. Claire County, Michigan, seems to be as wide as an ocean. Photograph by Darryl R. Beers.

11

REALM OF THE BAREFOOT BOY

Brian F. King

When summer comes, my heart returns
To sunny lanes of childhood days
That wind through vales of trees and fern
Where dreams are mileposts by the way,
Where echo clear the whistled tunes
Of barefoot boys in love with June.

A BOY AND NATURE

Virginia Blanck Moore

A boy needs woods when he's growing up
And open fields and a stream—
A place to lie and look at the sky
On top of a hill and dream.

A boy needs freedom to roam the trails
That his own two feet have made,
To foster joyful adventuring
And a spirit unafraid.

A boy who's lucky enough to grow
Deep-rooted in nature's ways
Carries its lessons of peace and strength
Within him all of his days.

*In the Columbia River Gorge National Scenic Area in Oregon,
Eagle Creek winds its way through Mount Hood National Forest.
Photograph by Terry Donnelly/Donnelly Austin Photography.*

Praise

Alice E. Charles

For the light haze on the mountain
And the fair blue of the sky
Where fleecy clouds, like distant ships,
Are calmly sailing by;
For the wealth of ripened berries
Hidden in the grasses tall,
And the nameless charm of summer
That casts a spell on all;
For fresh dawns and dewy evenings
And the heat of the sultry noon;
For the morning songs of sparrows
And the thrush's vesper tune;
For the scent of countless blossoms
Borne upon the cooling breeze;
For the sounds of the busy mowers
And the drowsy hum of bees;
For all your gifts of beauty
Which charm the ear and eye,
We bring to you our truest praise,
O lovely summertime well-nigh.

Noon

Marel Brown

I pause and listen, sure that I hear
A bobwhite's call upon the hill,
The whirr of bees and locusts near—
Everything else is still.

In vibrant sun the peach turns red,
While cotton and corn grow tall;
Fat, dreamy cows in the maple's shade—
I'm sure I see them all.

The light turns green, the traffic moves,
I merge with the crowded street:
No longer standing in a field
Where memories are sweet.

Summer's Best

LaVerne P. Larson

Torrid months with skies of blue,
When summer reigns supreme
I bask in golden sunshine,
An answer to a dream.

The garden's in full bloom now
As all the countryside,
Sweet, abundant, rich, and green,
Sings out with joy and pride.

Bright laughter of the children
Is heard throughout the day,
As they enjoy each hour
Before it slips away.

I love to watch the sunset
And fireflies brightly glow;
The air is filled with magic
When evening breezes blow.

My heart is free and happy,
And life is so sublime,
As each new day embraces
The good old summertime.

Inset: Bright yellow day lilies are part of summer's golden treasure. Photograph by Jessie Walker.

Sipping cool lemonade outside by a field of day lilies is a perfect way to spend a summer afternoon's leisure time. Photograph by William H. Johnson.

The Meadowlark

Edith Shaw Butler

His song is golden—
It comes to me
From the topmost branch
Of the tall ash tree.
In ecstasy
He lifts his throat
And pours forth music,
Note by note.
For a lovely world,
A lovely day,
He sings his heart
And mine away.

To the Skylark

Henry Polk Lowenstein

The skylark in the lovely month of June,
As on and up it soars so blithe and free
On nimble wings with golden throat in tune,
Pours out its strains of sweetest melody.
There is no darkened cloud to dim its course,
Nor angry storm its trustful hopes to blight;
It draws its power from that Mysterious Source
That fills the world with Law and Love and Light
And guides the mighty eagle in its flight.

Teach me, O God, the secret of its heart
When in the dazzling heights so near to Thee,
It still sends forth its flood of wondrous art
To fill the listening world with ecstasy;
And how this arbiter of boundless sky,
Along with Thee to guide its tiny brain,
Will fold its tireless wings without a sigh,
And, as my hopes and plans and efforts vain,
Like a falling star drop to the earth again.

This country garden in Floyd County, Indiana, is a beautiful gift of summer. Photograph by Daniel Dempster.

Hay and Honeysuckle Days

Alice MacKenzie Swaim

Do country lanes still hear cicadas sing
And lure with honeysuckle scent and hay,
To which drops of midsummer dew still cling,
As mockingbirds pour music down the way?
Do wild grapes twine around old pasture trees
And cows chew lazily on afternoons,
Heat-shimmering and murmurous with bees
That tick away the lavishness of Junes?
Do thistles ripen in untended fields
And orange lily chalices hold sun
While farmers cultivate rich harvest yields,
Then rock on porches when day's work is done?

Welcome, Honeysuckle

Georgia B. Adams

Swing wide the door of summer;
    The honeysuckle vine
Is sending forth aromas
    That hint of things divine.

As soon as the first blossom
    Opened its petals wide,
The bees were there and sharing
    The honey tucked inside.

Along the country fences
    These creamy blossoms trail;
Their sweet perfume is wafted
    All through the hill and dale.

The summer has arrived now;
    The honeysuckle's here
To spread its fragrant beauty
    And add a note of cheer.

Inset: This tempting honeysuckle blossom exudes its sweet perfume in Georgetown, South Carolina. Photograph by William H. Johnson.

Scarlet honeysuckle blooms gracefully in a summer garden. Photograph by Gay Bumgarner.

Wild Royalty

Jeanette Beem

There's a queen on Iowa's roadways,
So pure and humble white.
You will see her friendly waving
In the summer's sunny light.

Her beauty is of royalty;
Her castle is the home
She found along the byways
With the blue sky as her dome.

Her delicate white flowers
Adorn her head with grace,
As if they were selected
From the finest of all lace.

She will never win a prize
Or be judged in fancy shows,
But what better place to be,
For that is what God chose.

Whatever is her fate,
As each warm summer passes,
She returns in all her glory
And waves in tall, green grasses.

So when you roam the roadways
Of Iowa so fair,
May you take a second glance;
Queen Anne is standing there.

Wishes

Jessie Cannon Eldridge

I think that a young girl should wear
A crisp, bright ribbon in her hair;
That every summer day should grace
Its loveliness with Queen Anne's lace;
That flowering apple trees should hold
A robin's voice of liquid gold;
That on a long stone fence should run
One fat, gray squirrel, just for fun;
That night, when darkness daylight bars,
Should wear a diadem of stars.

Queen Anne's lace rules over the fields of summer. Photograph by Darryl R. Beers.

Haying Time
Dorothy Taggart

Fields starred over with daisies,
The grazing of his whetstone
Across the long crescent blade;
The easy, measured rhythm
Of his swing as the grass fell;
Air fragrant with the scent
    of new-mown hay;
The sweet tremolo of a
Melancholy tune he whistled;
The mild warmth of June sun
In an azure blue sky,
Not clear, but holding on high;
Great milk-white cumulus clouds
Sailing like ancient galleons,
Their dark shadows fast moving
Over the land where he mowed.

Alfalfa
Margaret Neel

I still remember—
Out on the farm,
In the late afternoons
When the sun was warm—
The pasture gate
That let me through
To the place
Where tall alfalfa grew—
Alfalfa, green
And lush and sweet,
And the ground so cool
To small bare feet.

I still remember
The sun going down,
Spilling pure gold
On the roofs of the town;
The clang of milk pails;
The cattle lowing;
And the cool, sweet fragrance
Of alfalfa growing.

Clover Field
Ruth B. Field

Nothing's more sweet than a red clover field
Caressed by the wind and kissed by the rain;
Redolent with dreams, here rich honey yield
Is garnered by bees where sunshine has lain.
Red clover nodding and white clover swayed
By plush bumblebees, zigzagging on wings
Like gossamer rainbows, through the blooms wade;
For deep in the clover the summertime sings.
In the green meadows that sway in a dance
To musical strains from ribbon-flung streams
Lies the fresh clover; its scent can entrance
With visions of beauty from tiptoeing dreams.
Over green clover the summer breeze cleaves
To lucid gold air where butterflies shine;
Magical alchemy, its subtle spell weaves
Tranquil content into patterns benign.
Breathe the rare fragrance; its essence unfolds
Within the heart's archives, always to keep.
Touch plush rose blossoms, their rapture behold
When they have vanished in long, silent sleep.
Freshened by night dew, the clover field glows
With words unspoken and poetry unsung;
But here something whispers, that the soul knows,
And lingers forever, where clover has sprung.

A field of clover in bloom carpets this area near tall oaks. Photograph by Carr Clifton.

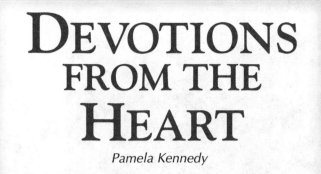

DEVOTIONS FROM THE HEART

Pamela Kennedy

Be patient, then, brothers, until the Lord's coming.
See how the farmer waits for the land to yield its valuable crop
and how patient he is for the autumn and spring rain. —James 5:7 (NIV)

WAITING FOR GOD

I can't wait until I graduate and I'm finally free from all these rules and regulations!" One of my frustrated high school students regaled her classmates with the latest version of adult injustice and misunderstanding.

"It seems like we will never have a family!" A young wife shared her concerns with a friend over a cup of coffee in the church fellowship hall between services on Sunday.

"Do you think my Sam will ever regain the strength he lost from the stroke?" An anxious woman grasped the hand of her physician when they met in the grocery store.

It seems everywhere I turn, there are people worried about when the Lord is going to visit them with the answers to their prayers. As I write this, our two sons are looking for better job opportunities; and our daughter is facing college graduation with questions about how she will manage in the "real world." We are concerned about how we can help our aging parents when they live thousands of miles away. We are in prayer over all these things; but waiting, as I often say, is not my best subject.

The apostle James was a man who spent time in the presence of the Lord, but he was no stranger to waiting either. He was a fisherman before Jesus called him and his brother Peter to become disciples. Certainly he had spent long hours waiting for fish to fill his nets. Then, after becoming a follower of Jesus, he had to learn to wait in a new way. It took patience to think differently; to forgive, instead of taking revenge; to

---

Prayer: Dear Heavenly Father, please help me to place my future in Your hands, waiting patiently until You make Your presence known through answered prayer.

---

withhold judgment; to listen; and to be obedient.

After the death and resurrection of Jesus, James still needed patience to wait for the coming of the Holy Spirit and later to accept his new role as a leader instead of being just a follower. By the time he wrote the words above, James was shepherding the congregation of Christian believers in Jerusalem. He had to be patient with the many problems that arose from such a position of leadership. I wonder how many times earnest Christians asked him how long they must suffer the persecution of Rome, deal with discrimination, or live in fear and poverty.

None of us likes to wait for the things we feel the Lord could be doing in our lives, yet waiting is often the very tool God uses to bring about the answers to our prayers. Just like the farmer, cited in the verse on the opposite page, we need to look at the rains of both autumn and spring as important factors in providing the fruit we desire. The farmer knows that the crops cannot be rushed, that seasons come and go, that both rain and sunshine have a part in producing the harvest for which he hopes.

Our lives are not so different. Patience is required because growth and change may take time. Like the farmer, we control neither the rain nor the growth; and although we have the privilege of taking part in the planting process, it is the Lord who is responsible for the results. But we can wait in patience because we know that in the end, the Lord does come. He will bring us the answers we seek, the grace we lack, the resolution we desire. The harvest of an anxious and worried farmer yields no more than that of a patient one. But as he waits, the patient farmer

Day lilies decorate the area near a barn in Shiawassee County, Michigan. Photograph by Darryl R. Beers.

experiences the joyful expectation that comes only from trusting in the Lord.

Pamela Kennedy is a freelance writer of short stories, articles, essays, and children's books. Wife of a retired naval officer and mother of three children, she has made her home on both U.S. coasts and currently resides in Honolulu, Hawaii.

Overleaf: Balsam root and lupine bloom in Tom MCall Nature Preserve on Rowena Crest above the Columbia River in Oregon. Photograph by Mary Liz Austin.

Grandmother's Helper

Joy Belle Burgess

I was Grandmother's little helper
And worked busily at her side;
Her kitchen hummed to the tempo
Of a crackling fire and canning time.
Dry fir and cedar snapped with glee
Inside the firebox's warm glow,
While the water rose, boiled, and steamed
In her copper boiler on the stove.
I washed two rows of small-mouthed jars
Until they sparkled, just like new.
And then I snapped baskets of string beans;
She watched, smiling at what I could do.
When the beans were scalded, cooled,
    and packed
Into her quart jars close and tight,

She reached for a little open crock
And let me salt the beans, just right.
Then into her bubbling boiler
She lowered jars on a long, wire rack
While I lingered and tidied the kitchen
Or read cookbooks and old almanacs.
And my efforts were well rewarded
By the sparkle in Grandmother's eye
When she gazed at the resplendent store
In her cellar, then gave a happy sigh.
Oh, how dear are all the memories,
Summers spent by my grandmother's side,
When her kitchen hummed
    and sang softly
Of our fulfillment at canning time.

Canning Time

Ruth B. Field

I kneel on warm ground by loaded rows
Of small green peas that my garden grows,
Feeling a kinship with summer and God
Each time I pick a ripe, green pod.
In my kitchen, I hull away
The covering from my food bouquet,
Exposing small jewels of sparkling hue,
Bits of warm sunshine and parts of dew
That shimmer like jade in a showcase.
Canning green peas is not commonplace
But something like conquering Venus or Mars,
When I store the summer away in clear jars.

*Bright bounty of summer, sunflowers and pickled peaches make a
cheerful, casual arrangement. Photograph by Nancy Matthews.*

Blueberry Time
Ruth B. Field

It's blueberry time on the pasture hills
Across mossy hummocks, where birds dip low.
Here, bright summer sunshine its warm gold spills
On dusty thistles, where steeplebush grows.

On a midsummer day, climb pasture bars,
Follow the cow path past great mullein spires,
Or wade through the daisies like fallen stars,
And then circle the milkweeds' tall spiked fires.

Here where the berries hang blue, sweet, and lush,
We pick them and drop them into our pails—
Huge clusters dangle from each swelling bush;
Ripe fruit falls on tin like a storm of hail.

Summer day here on the green pasture slopes
Where happily pass the long golden hours—
Old straw hats and a few hundred hopes,
With joy intermingled in leafy bowers;
Of muffins and jam and blueberry pies,
Fragrant and brown with rich juices oozing;
Fritters, flummery, some sweet surprise—
These are the blueberries for first choosing.
Laughter and sunshine, pails brimming over,
And back down the hill at the day's calm wane,
We stagger home through the crimson clover,
Lips telling tales with their blueberry stain.

Blue Buttons
Cecil B. Smith

Sweet memories of childhood and pleasures I knew
When summer was special and berries were blue.
Like tiny blue buttons on a miniature tree,
A branch of blueberries was charming to me.
How lovely to wander far back o'er a hill
And pick blueberries, my kettle to fill.
Then home o'er the hill my treasure I'd take,
And Mother would bake me a blueberry cake.
Some folks may not like it, but to me 'twas a treat—
So special each summer when berries were sweet.
A pie is delicious and easy to make;
But remembering Mother, I'll have blueberry cake.

Blackberrying
Vilet Bennett

All on a cloudless afternoon
We walked into the drowsy June.
Through meadows wide, across a stile,
We must have walked a country mile
Into a leafy, whispering wood
Where tree-sentinel soldiers stood.
Searching bushes low we found
Luscious berries near the ground,
Hanging there in clusters neat,
Tantalizing, purple-sweet.
We picked and ate some, saved some too.
See! Our hands are purple-blue.

Blueberries turn the fields a rich purple in the Blueberry Barrens of Columbia, Maine. Photograph by William H. Johnson.

THROUGH MY WINDOW

Pamela Kennedy

LESSONS FROM THE BERRY PATCH

My ninety-year-old mother and I were reminiscing the other day. We do a lot of that now. It seems as her recollections of recent events become less accurate, her memories of times past sharpen into focus. We have discussed her childhood with her ten siblings, her courtship with my father, my youth, and the experiences of my now-grown children during their visits to Grandma's house. One day I realized that my mother's life can be measured in berry patches.

As a young girl growing up in Maple Valley, Washington, Mother's summers were spent outdoors catching frogs, building dams to create swimming holes in a nearby creek, and picking through tangles of blackberry vines for succulent fruit to fill her pail. My mother never lost her love of picking berries, both wild and "civilized" as she called them; and on summer mornings when I was young, we would head for the U-Pick Berry Patch. With the two of us kneeling side by side in the dust, gathering strawberries, mother would talk quietly. There were lessons to learn about planning ahead, the value of hard work, and enjoying the fruit of your labors (literally!). When we presented our berries for weighing, I smiled innocently at the field owner with juice-stained lips as I happily digested a goodly portion of his profits.

When I was older, Mother took me into the woods behind the local cemetery to pick in her favorite patch of wild blackberries. It was hard work. The berries were small and the vines were treacherous with needle-sharp thorns. Mother protected her hands and arms from scratches by cutting finger holes in the toes of old socks and then pulling the sock tops over the cuffs of her flannel shirt.

I recall the berry patches of my past with fondness.

Blackberries ripened in the summer heat, and I thought the whole process of berry picking was ridiculous. The woods were boring, the work tiring, and the thorns sharp! I wanted to be with my friends swimming at the lake and gossiping about the latest summer romances, not stuck in the woods in a sweaty flannel shirt, picking through berry brambles with my mother. Mother, however, considered it a great time to discuss the value of perseverance, of diligence, and of how good things come to those who wait. I knew she was not talking about blackberries.

After I married and had children, we moved often, living on a series of military bases, none of which was near a berry patch. I bought my jams and jellies at the commissary and made my pies with fruit from produce stands or the frozen food aisle. But one summer we ended up staying with my parents while my husband attended a navy training course. On a hot August afternoon, my six-year-old son burst through the back door covered from head to toe with brilliant purple juice.

"Gramma, you've got tons and tons of berries just growing for free down there by the big trees! Can I have a bucket?" His grin was a purple as his shirt.

"Sure honey," she replied, throwing me a meaningful look of triumph as she took his sticky hand and headed for the garage.

She had another opportunity to dispense berry-patch wisdom, and she wasn't going to let it pass. In the days that followed, the two of them gathered gallons of blackberries. She made pies and jelly and froze bag after bag of the sun-ripened fruit.

Now, as I hold her hand and we remember that summer, I recall the berry patches of my past with fondness. Back then, time was measured in quarts and gallons, boxes and flats. I wish now I could return with her to a summer rich with the fragrance of warm berries. I wish now I could recall all the things she told me, the things I had not wanted to hear when I was younger and impatient. I look at her white hair, curled so carefully; and I remember when, pulled askew by a prickly berry vine, dark brown tendrils escaped from under her cotton bandanna. My mother looks at me with a twinkle in her eye and smiles.

"You never did like to pick berries did you?"

"No," I admit, feeling a bit chastened even now.

"But you sure liked to eat them!" She laughed out loud; and I caught a glimpse of the girl she used to be, the one who chased frogs and ate handfuls of sweet wild berries.

We have just completed construction of a summer cabin on a piece of property given to us by my mother. At the back of the property there is a bank of weeds about eight feet high and seventy-five feet long. I have an idea.

"Do you know what we are going to plant on the hillside behind the cabin, Mom?" I ask.

She looks a bit puzzled. "Cabin?"

"The one we're building at the canal. You remember, I showed you the pictures?"

She thinks for a moment. "Oh, at the beach. Where we used to go?"

"That is the place. I am going to plant huckleberry bushes and blueberries too. We will have our own berry patch, Mom."

"That is good." She squeezes my hand again and chuckles. "You could still learn a lot from spending a little time in a berry patch, honey."

Original artwork by Doris Ettlinger.

33

FAMILY RECIPES

CHOCOLATE STRAWBERRY DELIGHT

Lewis Wilkins, Maryville, Washington

1 package chocolate cake mix
1 3.9-ounce package chocolate
   instant pudding
1 8-ounce package cream cheese,
   softened

1 12-ounce package non-dairy
   topping
1 quart strawberries
1 13½-ounce package strawberry
   glaze

Preheat oven to 350°F. In a large bowl, prepare cake mix according to package directions. Turn batter into an 11- x 15-inch baking pan. Bake 25 minutes or until toothpick inserted into center comes out clean. Cool thoroughly on a wire rack. In a medium bowl, follow the instructions for the pie filling on the pudding mix box. Whip softened cream cheese into the pie mixture; spread over cake. Spread non-dairy topping over cream cheese. In a separate bowl, combine strawberries with glaze; spread over topping. Chill 2 hours to set. Makes 16 servings.

EASY NUTTY BLUEBERRY PIE

Sigrid R. Hice, Hickory, North Carolina

2 cups blueberries
1 cup granulated sugar, divided
1 tablespoon cinnamon
1 cup flour
1 teaspoon baking powder
⅛ teaspoon salt

2 eggs, lightly beaten
¼ cup vegetable oil
1 teaspoon vanilla
4 tablespoons milk
½ cup chopped pecans

Preheat oven to 350°F. Pour blueberries into an 8- x 8-inch pie plate. Mix one tablespoon each of sugar and cinnamon; sprinkle over blueberries. In a large mixing bowl, combine remaining sugar, flour, baking powder, and salt. Add eggs, oil, milk, and vanilla, stirring to mix thoroughly. Fold in pecans. Pour mixture over blueberries. Bake for 45 minutes. Makes 8 servings.

RASPBERRY PIE

Dora Henry, Springdale, Arkansas

1 cup water
2 tablespoons cornstarch
½ cup granulated sugar
⅛ teaspoon salt
1 tablespoon butter

1 3-ounce package raspberry
  sugar-free gelatin
1 pint raspberries
1 8-inch prebaked pie shell
1 cup heavy cream, whipped

In a small saucepan, combine water, cornstarch, salt, and sugar. Bring to a boil, stirring to dissolve sugar. Add butter; stir in raspberry gelatin and mix well. Remove from heat and fold in raspberries. Cool mixture for a few minutes and pour into prepared crust. Refrigerate pie until set. Just before serving, spoon whipped cream around edge of pie, allowing some raspberry filling to show in the center. Makes 8 servings.

BLUEBERRY CAKE

Linda Giles, Boothbay, Maine

½ cup butter
¾ cup, plus 1 tablespoon
  granulated sugar, divided
¼ teaspoon salt
1 teaspoon vanilla

2 eggs, separated
1½ cups, plus 1 tablespoon flour
1 teaspoon baking powder
⅓ cup milk
2 cups blueberries

Preheat oven to 350°F. In a medium bowl, cream butter with ½ cup sugar; add salt, vanilla, and egg yolks. Beat until light and creamy. Sift 1½ cups flour with baking powder. Add alternately with milk to mixture. Sprinkle 1 tablespoon flour over the berries and add to batter; set aside. Beat egg whites until foamy, gradually add ¼ cup sugar, beating to stiff peaks. Fold in egg whites. Pour into a greased and floured 8- x 8-inch pan. Sprinkle top with 1 tablespoon sugar. Bake for 50 minutes or until toothpick inserted into the center comes out clean. Makes 8 servings.

Even if you purchase your summer berries from a roadside stand, the pleasure of serving these wonderful desserts to your family and friends is still yours. Share the incredible taste of summer with these recipes from Ideals' readers. We would love to try your recipe too. Send a typed copy to Ideals Publications, 535 Metroplex Drive, Suite 250, Nashville, Tennessee 37211. Payment will be provided for each recipe published.

TWO BUTTERFLIES
Emily Dickinson

Two butterflies went out at noon
And waltzed above a stream,
Then stepped straight through
    the firmament
And rested on a beam;

And then together bore away
Upon a shining sea,—
Though never yet, in any port,
Their coming mentioned be.

MAGIC FLOWERS
Jill Noblit MacGregor

Bright butterflies,
Like pretty colored fans,
Flutter through the sky
Clapping their hands.
With big bright spots
On wings of chiffon,
Like little magic flowers
They light on the lawn.

SUMMER IN THE VALLEY
P. F. Freeman

Summer has reached the valley now;
In hives the bees are swarming;
The weeder has replaced the plow;
The weather's fair and warmer.
In green-tinged orchards, limbs hang low
From luscious fruits they are bearing;
Out in the garden, flowers grow;
There is beauty everywhere.

O'er grass bordering a winding lane,
A soft blanket has spread
Where tiny violets bloom again,
Near fenceposts up ahead.

The scented pines on yonder hill
Give fragrance down below;
Lush ferns are nodding by the rill
Where birch and willow grow.

In fields and meadows I can hear
The bluebirds as they sing—
Their melody is soft and clear,
As summer news they bring.
Deep in the wood's secluded bowers,
All natural life will rally
When it's summer in the valley.

A wicker chair offers a moment of relaxation in this country garden. Photograph by Gay Bumgarner.

The Lark Is Up to Meet the Sun

William Holmes McGuffey

The lark is up to meet the sun,
The bee is on the wing,
The ant its labor has begun,
The woods with music ring.
Shall birds and bees and ants be wise,
While I my moments waste?
O let me with the morning rise
And to my duty haste.

The Honeybee

C. M. Montgomery

'Cross sunlit field and meadow green,
The tiny honeybee,
In shafts of light may be seen
Winging over the lea.
Or yonder distant mountain peak
May beckon him to roam
On alpine slope, its pollen seek,
And fetch its nectar home.
Clover, hayfield, scented sage
He samples and moves on,
In Nature's book to write his page
Before the summer's gone.

Sing-Song

Christina Georgina Rossetti

Hurt no living thing:
Ladybird, nor butterfly,
Nor moth with dusty wing.

There are certain pursuits which, if not wholly poetic and true,
do at least suggest a nobler and finer relation to nature than we know.
The keeping of bees, for instance.

—Henry David Thoreau

Daises and black-eyed Susans provide the perfect feast for honeybees. Photograph by Jessie Walker.

BITS & PIECES

I'd be a butterfly born in a bower,
Where roses and lilies and violets meet.
—*Thomas Haynes Bayly*

*S*o work the honeybees,
Creatures that by a rule in nature teach
The act of order to a peopled kingdom.
—*William Shakespeare*

*T*he pedigree of Honey
Does not concern the Bee.
—*Emily Dicksinson*

*W*ild honey smells of freedom.
—*Anna Akhmatova*

*M*y banks they are furnish'd with bees,
Whose murmur invites one to sleep.
—*William Shenstone*

Books are the bees which carry the quickening
pollen from one to another mind.

—James Russell Lowell

Crowds of bees are giddy with clover,
Crowds of grasshoppers skip at our feet,
Crowds of larks at their matins hang over,
Thanking the Lord for a life so sweet.

—Jean Ingelow

Butterflies . . . not quite birds, as they were not
quite flowers, mysterious and fascinating as are all
indeterminate creatures.

—Elizabeth Goudge

For where's the state beneath the firmament
That doth excel the bees for government?

—Guillaume de Salluste Du Bartas

41

BACKYARD CALENDAR

Joan Donaldson

The afternoon shower has moistened the soil so that the perfume of damp earth greets me when I enter my garden. A few scattered clouds skim the evening sky. June is a month full of softness, from the slanted golden rays to the grass beneath my bare feet. Beads of moisture linger on the furry leaves of a sage plant and on the petals of blue clematis. These mild days slip into balmy evenings, perfect for a few minutes of solitude. I know that too soon the dog days of July will crisp the grass and bake the soil.

But on this mellow evening, I check the rain gauge and am thankful for the spate of showers. I can weed a bit and enjoy the collage of colors and scents. Although setting out bedding plants hastens the results for a northern gardener, there is nothing as satisfying as planting seeds and measuring the results.

Now squash vines creep between the stalks of corn that reach skyward. In the center of the corn plants rests a pool of collected rainwater. A couple of honeybees sip from the sun-warmed water before pollinating the green beans. Just as I find refreshment from the texture of dill or the scent of basil, bees come to this sanctuary for nourishment.

The evening call of the cardinal and the dimming light remind me that I have come for strawberries. I kneel and search beneath the leaves for the red treasures. Already these plants have provided numerous quarts of fruit, now frozen away. Some snowy morning, I will blend them into smoothies and taste again these June days when strawberries appear at every meal. But I love the berries best when they are warm from the sun and full of sugar. I nibble as I drop the fruit into my bucket. These pleasant moments are the hidden riches that propel a gardener to plant and mulch. Only one who works the soil can taste such fruit.

Strawberry

The fragrance of roses mingles with the scent of strawberries as I come to the end of the berry bed. Just as strawberries fill our bowls, old roses reign in June. Their fragrance lingers in the moist air where the border is laden with blossoms. Rich maroon, deep pink, and pale ivory petals shimmer in the twilight. Pulling scissors from my pocket, I snip a bouquet. Even though these cut roses will only perfume my home for a day before they drop their petals, I still bring them inside. June may bring the longest days of the year; but these seasonal pleasures slide by too quickly, so I gather them now.

The evening star glows in the west where lavender shades the sky. The clouds have moved eastward. Picking up my bucket of berries, I close the garden gate, grateful for the sweetness of this small sanctuary.

Joan Donaldson is the author of a picture book and a young adult novel, as well as essays that have appeared in many national publications. She and her husband raised their sons on Pleasant Hill Farm in Michigan, where they continue to practice rural skills.

A garden path is bordered by lovely blossoms of summer.
Photograph by Terry Donnelly/Donnelly Austin Photography.

Flower Memories
Lucille Crumley

Geraniums remind me
Of a cottage I once knew
With its long, front porch
Where the blazing flowers grew;

Of shining little windowpanes,
With quaint lace curtains showing;
Of summertime and porch swings;
On lines, clean clothes a-blowing;

Of a child with summer dreams;
Of sunshine on a wooden floor.
Geraniums remind me
Of a house with open door.

Red Geraniums
Martha Haskell Clarke

Life did not bring me silken gowns,
Nor jewels for my hair,
Nor signs of gabled foreign towns
In distant countries fair;
But I can glimpse, beyond my pane, a green and friendly hill
And red geraniums aflame upon my windowsill.

The brambled cares of everyday,
The tiny humdrum things,
May bind my feet when they would stray;
But still my heart has wings
While red geraniums are bloomed against my window glass
And low above my green-sweet hill the gypsy wind-clouds pass.

And if my dreamings ne'er come true,
The brightest and the best,
But leave me lone my journey through,
I'll set my heart at rest
And thank God for home-sweet things, a green and friendly hill
And red geraniums aflame upon my windowsill.

This vine-covered entrance to a potter's studio is fronted by a large container garden exhibiting zinnias, daisies, and other flowers. Photograph by Jessie Walker.

READERS' REFLECTIONS

Readers are invited to submit original poetry for possible publication in future issues of IDEALS. *Please send typed copies only; manuscripts will not be returned. Writers receive payment for each published submission. Send material to Readers' Reflections, Ideals Publications, 535 Metroplex Drive, Suite 250, Nashville, Tennessee 37211.*

Sunflower Sunshine
Stacy Smith
Anderson, Indiana

Where violas shyly peek their heads,
Yellow suns tower overhead
With bursts of petals glowing bright
And leaves dappled in summer's light.

The birds planted them for me
And picked the spot so perfectly,
Where they grow with golden grace
Amid other hues in the garden space.

When they're equal to the weeds,
I'll gather up the blackened seeds
And offer them to those that fed
And brought sunshine to my flowerbed.

Wildflowers
Arline Lambert
Bozeman, Montana

Raising bright faces beneath the trees,
Wafting their scent on the gentle breeze,
Glowing in sunlight, shade, or rain,
Lifting my spirits again and again
Are God's little flowers, planted there
To spread His beauty, to tell of His care,
A light to the eye,
A joy to the heart,
Ever so shy
But ever a part
Of making life glad, relieving its pain.
I touch, oh, so gently; once, then again—
But leave their sweet message for others to see.
These precious wildflowers are not just for me!

Treasure Hunt

Goldie Counts
White Marsh, Maryland

I like to rise at crack of dawn
And sit quietly for a while
With thoughts set free to wander
Across the years and miles.
I do not know where they will go
Nor what treasures they will find.
I only know they often seek
The back roads of my mind.
Sometimes they choose a moss-green path
Where wintergreen and laurel grow;
Sometimes freshly-hoed furrows
Where corn stands, row on row;
Sometimes they find a weathered wall
Where rambling roses cling;

Sometimes they taste sweet water
From a clear, cold mountain spring.
Then they come winging back to me
O'er wooded hills and sleepy farms.
They place the treasures they have found
Into my waiting arms.
I hold them close, then one by one
With the sun's first golden ray,
Through my open window
I watch them fly away.
Then I count my many blessings
As I bow my head to pray,
I thank God for treasured memories,
And the promise of a bright new day.

Summertime

Debra J. Butler
Gahann, Ohio

Lush, green foliage grasps bare tree limbs;
Vibrant, gold sunflowers pose on tall, thick stems.
Twinkling fireflies gleam in the twilight;
A radiant sunset flaunts beauty so bright.
The season of summer has begun,
Alive with dreams of pleasure and fun.
Fresh smell of cut grass begins growth anew;
A cardinal swoops down dressed in scarlet-red hue.
The humming of crickets serenade with their sound,
While swarms of honeybees zip and hover around.

Fireworks boom on the Fourth of July;
A rainbow of color splashes the sky.
The taste of watermelon, luscious and sweet,
A perfect refreshment in smoldering heat.
Fishermen drift in their boats on a lake,
Eager to cast their lines at daybreak.
Sunshine stays longer into the night,
Warming the air with fervent delight.
The season of summer has begun,
Alive with dreams of pleasure and fun.

SLICE OF LIFE
Edna Jaques

HOME RELISH

There is a sweet nostalgic charm
    About an old country farm
That pulls your heart strings all awry—
    A clean breathtaking sweep of sky;
An old gray barn built on a knoll;
    A young mare nuzzling at her foal;

A blue jay scolding like a shrew;
    A row of cedars faintly blue
Against the misty skyline—where
    Small clouds are hanging in midair,
Like blankets on a crazy line,
    Above the rows of dark blue pine.

There is a woodshed and a pump,
    An old tan rooster getting plump
From the rich fare about the yard
    Where an old collie dog stands guard
And growls at anyone who dares
    To come upon him unaware.

Far from the city's hectic pace,
    The people on this country place
Are peaceful as a summer night.
    Their windows send out beams of light,
While the old farmhouse stands four-square
    To guard the people living there.

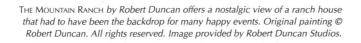

Summer Days

Shirley Sallay

I stand here before the homestead
That we as youngsters knew;
I see the scenes of yesteryear
Come bobbing into view.
How I loved the days of summer
When changes came about
That left no time for loneliness
Or sorrowing or doubt.

I loved the early morning sun;
Fresh buds with dewdrops in their eyes;
Richly fragrant, balmy breezes
Waltzing o'er the cloudless skies;
Butterflies dancing over flowers;
The buzz of bees upon a rose;
A streamlet bubbling o'er the rocks,
Beneath green willows in repose.

We children raced through waving fields
Of daisies blooming bright
And went to bed when cricket songs
Broke through the mist of night.
Sweet aromas from the kitchen,
Where Grandma made the jam,
Blend with thoughts of the swimming hole
Where we, for hours, played.

Soap-making day, the kettle hung
Above a fire outdoors;
Each one of us was asked to help
With morn and evening chores.
Each summertime when I return
Recalling days of yore,
I still see our old home and friends,
Just as they were before.

*Hollyhocks stand tall in front of the Little Studio at
Saint-Gaudens National Historic Site in Cornish, New
Hampshire. Photograph by William H. Johnson.*

On the Veranda
Inez Baker

When summer sun beat down outside
In brassy, breathless glare,
No clouds appeared to mute the blue,
No breezes stirred the air.
Then children tired of jumping rope
Or playing in the sand;
Too hot, it seemed, for riding bikes
When metal burned the hand.
'Twas then our mother called to us
To come up in the shade,
And there for many hours at games
Of school or store we played.
It seemed those days that everything
Grew silent from the heat,
Except the bees that gently buzzed
In nearby fields of wheat.
And as the day was slowing down,
Relaxing its fast pace,
Life on the wide veranda
Was the best of any place.

The Old Porch Swing
Mrs. Gene Sharon Smith

I love to sit at twilight time
Out in the old porch swing,
Savoring all the scents of night;
Hearing the crickets sing;
Swaying slowly, back and forth,
Thinking of yesterday;
Listening to laughing children
When they're called home from play.
This world has much to entertain,
But surely there's not one thing
That brings more peace
    and comfort than to
Sit in an old porch swing.

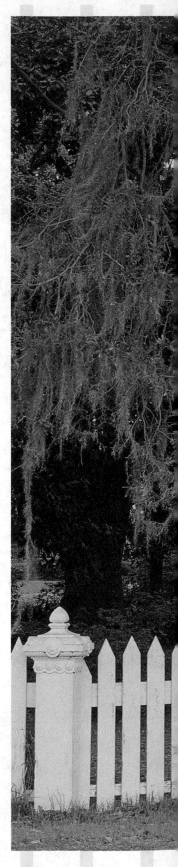

"Porch-sitting" has almost become a forgotten art. . . . To behold the wonder of God's world, to revel in its grandeur, to recognize that this world has been given us to enjoy—these are the benefits from porch-sitting. Another follows: that of being together. The usual pace of activities all too often separates us as families.

How necessary, then, that there be times when we become reacquainted with those we love best. Then, porch-sitting has the inevitable consequence of conversation. This is more than talk. It is the sharing of experiences, ideas, feelings. It is the freedom to express those thoughts which lie deep in the heart. Let me recommend to you the art of porch-sitting.

—James E. Fogartie

Spanish moss sways gently in the breezes at Tezcuco Plantation in Darrow, Louisiana. Photograph by William H. Johnson.

Farmers' Picnic

Ralph W. Seager

No matter which day of the week Farmers' Picnic came on, it was the best Sunday in the year. The hours of this day defied all clocks, for each one held a week's worth of time. A boy cheats his birthday at Farmers' Picnic. He lives twice over in one day and never forgets it.

I never knew it to rain on the day of the Farmers' Picnic; the heavens had better sense than to disrupt this best of country celebrations. The chores were stepped up early in the morning. The cows went straight to their stanchions; and the horses gave way to the sides of their stalls, and no crowding. The chickens came at the first rattle of the pan and the pigs were at the trough. It was all business and no nonsense. Farmers' Picnic came only once a year.

By breakfast, everything was spick-and-span. Ears got a second going over. Hair that had been tossed all summer by hay-drying breezes put up a stiff resistance to steel-toothed combs, and no amount of sticking could maintain discipline. A small boy's rebellion came right out through his cowlick. At last we were all pinched into our best clothes, starched, ribboned, and shined.

The picnics were usually held in the schoolyard, although some of the events took place in Botsford's Grove, just a piece away and across the road. Folks would begin to show up from nine o'clock on.

Grownup neighbors, near and far, made islands in a sea of children. Farmers carefully untied long cornstalks from their rigs and set them against the schoolhouse to see who had raised the tallest. Another farmer would reach under a buggy seat and, with a ten-fingered pride, lift out his prize clutch of early potatoes—smooth, red, and all-of-a-size. It was country fair all right—everything blue ribboned.

Every home freezer in the valley was put into service in the maple grove beside the school. The custard came farm-fresh in milk cans with linen towels caught under the lids to prevent spilling. Wash tubs full of ice packed in sawdust were unloaded, and we boys chipped away with our jackknives and ran wild with pieces of Sugar Creek in our mouths. I always felt proud about the ice because it came from our barn where my father had buried these January diamonds in a deep mow of sawdust.

At the schoolyard, six or seven handles were being turned at once: salt and ice—ice and salt. Turn with the left hand—more ice; turn with the right—more salt. Sugar Creek gave up its sweetness and became brine, and the plug hole in the freezer's side ran full. The custard thickened, the handles slowed, and arms ached—but such a delicious ache. When a boy put two hands to the handle, the experts knew it was enough, the magic had been wrought. As the dashers were brought up out of those jubilees of vanilla, chocolate, or lemon, long spoons scraped them partly clean and the quick tongues of boys and girls did the rest. If there is a better benediction for young, hot throats than old-fashioned lemon custard ice cream, the world has not yet discovered it.

Our Farmers' Picnic had a parade with wild animals and brass bands in it. Upon the hay rig that served as the bandwagon were my father with his brass valve trombone, my uncle and his nickel-plated cornet, and other men—a chariot-load of Gabriels. They knew only one march, but they knew it loudly. After them came the giraffe, or

Summer flowers spill out of a red watering can flanked by a prize-winning pie and fresh fruit. Photograph by Nancy Matthews.

and-take as families and forks, plates and parents, were shuffled around. The long tables sagged with cold smoked hams; fried chicken, crusty and golden; homemade bread that swelled out of the tins with pride; ripe cucumber pickles; potato salad; cornbread and clover butter; and deviled eggs. Handprints of strawberry jams were soon showing on the fronts of little dresses and lemonade splatter down the sleeves of shirts.

The men pitched horseshoes, laid straws against the close ones, and measured every point. The younger ones went to the field next to the marsh, and a ball game was soon under way.

The boys had a race from the schoolyard fence to the closest mailbox. A farmer showed us a big white rabbit that would be the prize. All I knew about running was to stand up and go—and when the starter yelled "Go," I went. I ran like the time I knocked the hornet nest out of the pear tree. I raised as much dust as when a bull got out and chased me down this same road all the way home. I became a cousin to that rabbit as I skipped and bobbed and jumped along the rutted road.

Now it was nearing chore time. The wagons were packed, goodbyes said, and the committee announced for next year's picnic. On my lap was a burlap bag with life in it; and during the evening ride home, I slipped my hand down the open end and gently wound my fingers around two long ears. The whole day belonged to me.

"gyraffey" as our neighbor would say. Here was my animal storybook come to life, but it walked strangely. Sometimes his back end sashayed around until it came ahead of his front end. It would get its feet mixed up, coming cross-legged.

The schoolchildren marched in the parade; and buggies with daisies woven into solid wheels were driven by pretty girls. When the parade rattled across Botsford's Bridge, the women folk turned to the table of food and began to organize for the best feast this side of Canaan. It was give-

FOR THE CHILDREN

To My Kittens

Eileen Spinelli

Mewing kittens
stay close by
to Mama Cat's
soft lullaby,
to mouse-y toys,
my old white sock,
the gentle ticking
of the clock.

There is a wider
world out there
beyond the rug
and rocking chair—
a world of fields
and creeks
and trees,
and one day
you'll explore
all these.

For now,
this is
the place to be—
a playful heap
delighting me.

Two buddies share a summer's task in this painting entitled SHUCKS *by Kathryn Andrews Fincher. Copyright © Kathryn Andrews Fincher. All rights reserved.*

FROM AMERICA'S ATTIC

D. Fran Morley and Maud Dawson

HERSHEY'S MILK CHOCOLATE CANDY BAR

On sunny afternoons, a small group of friends and I would make the hour-long walk home from elementary school. A few would race ahead, but more paused to take time to swing across a tributary of the town creek on an old tire. And others ambled behind, having been persuaded to hold the more gregarious ones' books for "just a minute." As a reward for bearing the weight of those books, but mostly just because it was a highlight of our week, we would often stop at the corner grocery store and count out our pennies for a five-cent Hershey's chocolate bar. Whoever did not have the required number of pennies would plead for a few squares from someone else's bar, and usually there would be one who would succumb and break off a perfect chocolate square or two for the beggar. I treasured the experience of one square of milk chocolate melting slowly on the tongue, as did most Americans.

Originally identified on its wrapper as "a nutritious confection," the chocolate bar with the three rows of four squares became the flagship product by which the Hershey Chocolate Company emerged as one of the most recognizable American institutions. Americans were able to indulge in the experience of eating milk chocolate, previously limited to wealthier Europeans, due to the vision of Pennsylvania businessman Milton S. Hershey.

In 1894, Hershey, with money from the sale of his Lancaster Caramel Company, established the Hershey Chocolate Company in his hometown of Derry Township. His first products were baking chocolate and cocoa powder. After experimenting with the basic recipe, Hershey, often seen in hip boots working long hours in his laboratory, created a formula for milk chocolate candy that had a dependable shelf life.

The Hershey's milk chocolate bar was introduced to the American public in 1900 in its standard two-ounce size, and its wrappers bore slogans such as "a sweet to eat, a food to drink" referring to the candy bar and the cocoa powder. At the time, calories were considered important to health, and since a pound of chocolate had more calories than a pound of meat, the slogan "more nutritious than meat" was often used.

A few years after introducing the chocolate bar, Hershey created the familiar "Hershey's Maroon" colored wrapping to go over the inner foil used to prevent the chocolate from

His Hand

Mary Newlin Roberts

My great-grandfather let me hold his hand
When I walked with him about the land.
I loved the way he used his stick
To poke at rocks and moles;
He showed me earthen runways
And where the snakes had holes.
And all the fields were daisies
And all the skies were blue—
For I was only seven
And he was seventy-two.
He took me also near the barn
To see the colt at play;
He took me up into the loft
Where the kittens slept in hay,
And he was very silent
While I chattered like a brook.

They tell me he was handsome
With a tall and noble look,
But the kind clasp of his fingers
Was all of him I knew—
For I was only seven
And he was seventy-two.

absorbing other flavors. During World War II foil was rationed and the inner wrapper was made of glassine. In the mid-1980s, the inner foil wrapper returned. Recently, the company began using the one-piece "fin" wrapper, so-called because the back seam forms the shape of a fin.

During the 1950s, inflation hit the cocoa bean market, and in order to keep the candy bar's five cent retail price, the company adjusted the candy bar's weight, the lowest being five-eighths of an ounce. Amazingly, the candy bar continued to be sold for a nickle until 1969.

The additional product that makes Hershey a familiar name is the popular silver foil-wrapped Kisses, introduced in 1907. Molded in the cone shape from the same milk chocolate as the candy bar, the product's trademarked paper plumes were included a few years later to distinguish Hershey®'s Kisses from imitators.

The Hershey®'s milk chocolate candy bar has helped spread goodwill across the globe. GIs shared their candy bars during World Wars I and II with civilians. During the Berlin Airlift, just after World War II, an Air Force pilot, Gail Halvorsen, included Hershey®'s bars in the relief packages he and his squadron dropped over the blockaded city. They "wiggled" the wings of their planes to signal the waiting children that the treats would soon be floating down. By 1949, more than 250,000 parachutes of candy had been

delivered to nearly 100,000 children in Berlin.

Milton Hershey would have approved of people using his milk chocolate to establish friendships. With his considerable personal fortune, he helped design and create a town, appropriately named Hershey, that included such elements as attractive housing, churches, parks, a community hall, a department store, a swimming pool, and even an amusement park and a zoo.

Although Hershey and his wife had no children, they began a school for underprivileged children that exists today and is supported by the foundation he established.

I am delighted that America adopted Milton Hershey's dream of a solid milk chocolate candy bar because around three o'clock each afternoon, I begin to think about a treat. Often that becomes the pleasure of one perfect square of milk chocolate melting on my tongue.

Images provided by Hershey Community Archives.

Father's World

Esther Kem Thomas

My father was one to
    stand at night
And look up at the sky
At springtime moons and
    blue starlight
And clouds that drifted by.
He seemed to drink the
    fragrant air
In natural, keen delight.
One with the breeze that
    stirred his hair,
He'd murmur, "Some nice night!"

My father was one to
    love the heat
Of any summer day;
The clover field to
    him was sweet;
He mowed it all away.
With shirt stuck to his
    back and wet,

Upon the hay he'd climb
And pause to mop his
    face and say,
"Ah, good old summertime."

My father was one who
    liked to live,
Who savored simple things.
He reached out, not to
    take, but give
And lent us strength for wings
To reach beyond our
    home and know
That his heart with us
    would always go
And that in the greens of
    trees and songs of birds
We could see and hear his
    gentle words.

Inset: Small wildflowers appear to raise their faces toward the sun in Kenosha, Wisconsin. Photograph by Darryl R. Beers.

Cumulus clouds float over a bunch grass prairie in Zumwalt Prairie Preserve, Oregon, part of a Nature Conservancy Preserve in Wallowa County. Photograph by Terry Donnelly/Donnelly Austin.

Father

Frances Frost

My father's face is brown with sun,
His body tall and limber.
His hands are gentle with beast or child
And strong as hardwood timber.

My father's eyes are the colors of sky,
Clear blue or gray as rain:
They change with the swinging change of days
While he watches the weather vane.

That galleon, golden upon our barn,
Veers with the world's four winds.
My father, his eyes on the vane, knows when
To fill our barley bins,

To stack our wood and pile our mows
With redtop and sweet tossed clover.
He captains our farm that rides the winds,
A keen-eyed, brown-earth lover.

*When tillage begins, other
arts follow. The farmers,
therefore, are the founders of
human civilization.*

—DANIEL WEBSTER

*Sunflowers parade their gregarious blooms
in front of a barn near Tawas Point, Michigan.
Photograph by Daniel Dempster.*

To the Boy

Edgar A. Guest

I have no wish, my little lad,
To climb the towering heights of fame.
I am content to be your dad
And share with you each pleasant game.
I am content to hold your hand
And walk along life's path with you
And talk of things we understand—
The birds and trees and skies of blue.

Though some may seek the smile of kings,
For me your laughter's joy enough;
I have no wish to claim the things
Which lure men into pathways rough.
I am happiest when you and I,
Unmindful of life's bitter cares,
Together watch the clouds drift by
Or follow boyhood's thoroughfares.

I crave no more of life than this:
Continuance of such a trust;
Your smile, whate'er the morning is,
Until my clay returns to dust.
If but this comradeship may last
Until I end my earthly task—
Your hand and mine by love held fast—
Fame has no charm for which I'd ask.

I would not trade one day with you
To wear the purple robes of power,
Nor drop your hand from mine to do
Some great deed in a selfish hour.
For you have brought me joy serene
And made my soul supremely glad.
In life rewarded I have been;
'Twas all worthwhile to be your dad.

The banks of Little Spokane River near Chattaroy in Spokane County, Washington, are dotted with yellow irises. Photograph by Mary Liz Austin/ Donnelly Austin Photography.

FATHER'S STORY

Elizabeth Madox Roberts

We put more coal on the big red fire,
    And while we wait for dinner to cook,
Our father comes and tells us about
    A story that he has read in a book.

And Charles and Will and Dick and I
    And all of us but Clarence are there.
And some of us sit on Father's legs,
    But one has to sit on the little red chair.

And when we are sitting very still,
    He sings us a song or tells a piece;
He sings "Dan Tucker Went to Town,"
    Or he tells us about the golden fleece.

He tells us about the golden wool;
    And some of it is about a boy
Named Jason, and about a ship;
    And some is about a town called Troy.

And while he is telling or singing it through,
    I stand by his arm, for that is my place.

To be honest, to be kind—to earn a little and to spend
a little less, to make upon the whole a family happier for
his presence, to renounce when that shall be necessary and
not to be embittered, to keep a few friends but these
without capitulation—above all, on the same grim
condition to keep friends with himself—here is a task for
all that a man has of fortitude and delicacy.

—ROBERT LOUIS STEVENSON

*A 1900s lantern, copper pots, and a cast-iron stove are part of
an old-fashioned country kitchen. Photograph by Jessie Walker.*

Letter to Martha Jefferson (Patsy) from Her Father

April 7, 1787

I have received letters which inform me that our dear Polly will certainly come to us this summer. By the time I return, it will be time to expect her. When she arrives, she will become a precious charge on your hands. The difference of your age, and your common loss of a mother, will put that office on you.

Teach her above all things to be good: because without that we can neither be valued by others, nor set any value on ourselves.

Teach her to be always true. No vice is so mean as the want of truth, and at the same time so useless.

Teach her never to be angry. Anger only serves to torment ourselves [and] to divert others and alienate their esteem.

And teach her industry and application to useful pursuits. I will venture to assure you that if you inculcate this in her mind you will make her a happy being in herself, a most estimable friend to you, and precious to all the world. In teaching her these dispositions of mind, you will be more fixed in them yourself and render yourself dear to all your acquaintance.

Practice them then, my dear, without ceasing. If ever you find youself in difficulty and doubt how to extricate yourself, do what is right, and you will find it the easiest way of getting out of the difficulty.

Do it for the additional incitement of increasing the happiness of him who loves you infinitely, and who is, my dear Patsy, yours affectionately,

—THOMAS JEFFERSON

Lupines and graceful grasses spread across Steptoe Butte, and the green hills of Washington stand majestically in the distance. Photograph by Mary Liz Austin/Donnelly Austin Photography.

I talk and talk and talk,
and I have not taught people
in fifty years what my
father taught by example
in one week.
—Mario Cuomo

To My Father

William Hamilton Hayne

It matters not that Time has shed
His thawless snow upon your head,
For he maintains, with wondrous art,
Perpetual summer in your heart.

None of you can ever be
proud enough of being the child
of such a father who has
not his equal in this world—
so great, so good, so faultless. . . .
Try, therefore, to be like him
in some points, and you will have
acquired a great deal.
—Queen Victoria

70

*Daisies are the centerpiece of this backyard garden in Algoma,
Wisconsin. Photograph by Darryl R. Beers.*

LETTERS FROM DADDY

In my first weeks as a college freshman, nothing pleased me more than finding a letter in my mailbox. Several times a day, I would make the trek across campus to the student center, hoping to find a note from a friend or relative. Letters from home helped give me confidence to reach out to new people, even as they helped me feel closer to the ones I had left behind. Eager to keep up with news from my hometown, I opened letters postmarked from Morristown immediately. Unless the letter was from my father.

Recognizing my father's script on the envelope, I would quickly tuck the letter into my backpack, afraid the tears welling in my eyes would betray my emotions. I was trying to be a mature and independent college girl, after all. But with just a glimpse of my father's handwriting, I was reduced to a homesick daddy's girl.

Growing up, I idolized my dad. He was a minister, and in my mind there was no Bible question that he could not answer. But even more impressive to me, he lived his faith. I knew he was a man devoted to prayer and Bible study because I saw that he communed with God daily. He served and counseled church members with patience and compassion, yet he never forsook his role as husband and father. He served God, church, and family with quiet humility. In my young eyes, he was perfect.

Heading back to my dormitory to read a letter from my father, I smiled remembering how Daddy's letters had helped take the edge off my homesickness during my first trips away from home. When my sister and I spent a week at summer camp together, Daddy wrote that he asked our younger brother if he missed us girls. "If the girls were here," three-year-old Nathan responded, "I would put them in the trash can." Only a brother could make you miss him more with such a statement.

Daddy's letters could always make me laugh. "I'm sorry I haven't taken time to write yet," he once wrote to me at camp. "We have been busy painting your room this week. It looks really nice.

I do not often enough tell you that I love you and appreciate you, but I really do.

I think you'll like the polka dots and stripes." Daddy often included comic strips, sometimes jotting notes relating to camp food or new friends.

My father used his letters as teaching tools also. "Thought you might enjoy this good article," he would casually suggest at the end of a letter. I still have many of the magazine clippings he sent me to encourage purity or strengthen my faith.

Most meaningful to me were Daddy's heartfelt sentiments. After I served as a counselor during the week he was camp director, he took the time to write me a letter. "Dear Melissa," he began, "I was so proud of you at camp again this year. You

A flower-bedecked mailbox makes retrieving the mail a pleasant event. Photograph by Nancy Matthews.

got involved, spent time with the campers, and made me proud in every way. I do not often enough tell you that I love you and appreciate you, but I really do. I am so glad to have you as my daughter. I hope this school year will be a great one for you. Learn just as much as you can, because these years will soon be gone. I love you with all my heart. Daddy." I treasure this letter and all the others I received from him.

Daddy's letters taught me the power of putting pen to paper. This is a lesson put into practice today. As my children make their first tentative steps into the world, I hope that a note slipped into their lunch boxes will help them get through kindergarten. As they grow, I hope that the letters I write along the way will encourage and teach them, but most of all remind them they are loved.

This year for Father's Day, I am sending Daddy a letter. I want him to know that after all these years, in my eyes he is still perfect. I hope that when he recognizes my familiar script on the envelope, he will know this letter is one to tuck into his heart to keep forever.

Melissa Lester is a freelance writer living in Wetumpka, Alabama, with her husband, two sons, and a daughter.

PARKERSBURG, WEST VIRGINIA

According to the calendar, summer begins on June 21 and ends on September 22; but when I was growing up in Parkersburg, West Virginia, summer started the day school was out and went on forever, or so it seemed. In those last years of the forties, the country was giddy with the promise of peace and prosperity. My father had come home from the war, and all was right with the world.

Young as we were, my sisters and my brother and I understood that Memorial Day and the Forth of July had new meaning. The four of us—dressed in red, white, and blue—marched in our own mini-parade around the City Park. After the speeches and the rides and the cotton candy, we sat quietly by the lily pond. Masses of pink and creamy white lilies floated on the still water. It was the biggest lily pond in the United States, my mother said; but I thought she must be wrong. How, I wondered, could little Parkersburg have the biggest of anything? But it was true. And it was beautiful.

One day, my uncle took us to Stewart Air Park, north of town, where a few Piper Cubs were lined up wing to wing. "Who wants to go for a ride?" he asked. Since my sisters and I had never known a time when tires and gasoline were not rationed, he might as well have suggested a journey to Oz.

The town where I had lived all my life looked so different from the air! The pilot made a couple of passes over our house, but all the houses looked the same to me. I could see the Ohio River and the lush green of Blennerhassett Island, where Aaron Burr and Harman Blennerhassett were accused of plotting to establish a separate nation in the Southwest. That flight was certainly the highlight of conversation for many summers.

Most days, though, we stayed close to home. We made boats, powered by rubber bands, and watched them zigzag around in an old washtub. Long-legged grasshoppers, shanghaied from our

---

I still live just a few miles north of where I was born.

---

sunny side yard, served as passengers and crew. The trouble was, we never figured out how to keep them from jumping ship.

When we became bored with boats and uncooperative insects, my two sisters and I retired to our "kitchen," an area near the garden that could always be counted on as a source of good "baking mix," or as adults mistakenly called it—mud. Using a set of old gelatin molds and outdated staples from the kitchen, my sisters and I created an array of pastries and placed them in the sun to bake. Decorated with clover blossoms, assorted weeds, and cupboard cast-offs, they

At one time described as the most beautiful home west of the Alleghenies, the Blennerhassett Mansion was completed in 1800 by Irishman Harman Blennerhassett. The house had approximately seven thousand square feet of floor space and more than two acres of gardens. Photograph courtesy of West Virginia State Parks.

almost looked good enough to eat.

We often baked until nightfall when the fireflies—we called them lightning bugs—appeared, flitting through the fragrant dusk. We collected them, placing them in Mason jars filled with grass so they would feel at home. We also enjoyed watching striped caterpillars turn into jade pendants that quivered when touched; or we picked handfuls of four-leaf clovers from a patch in our yard. Other days, we might be found roller-skating on the uneven concrete in front of the house or playing games like hide-and-seek and box hockey and sandlot ball.

Like all good things, the endless summer ended. As I grew older, summers zipped by like a video on fast-forward. Our world changed. The little airpark where we embarked on that magical journey was swallowed up by a mall. The magnificent lilies are gone, replaced by a modern sculpture fountain, ducks, and paddleboats. Blennerhassett Island is now a state park; and each year a stern-wheeler ferries nearly fifty thousand people to the island where they may picnic, shop, take horse-drawn wagon rides, and tour the rebuilt Blennerhassett mansion.

I still live just a few miles north of where I was born. It is quite wonderful to contemplate the changes that have taken place in the last half century. Yet, in my heart, I know those endless summers in our small town were indeed the best of times.

Since retiring, Patsy Evans Pittman's stories, poems, and essays have appeared in a variety of women's and inspirational publications, as well as several anthologies. She and her husband Stanley enjoy travel, but they are always glad to get back to their home.

It is now the moment when by common consent we pause to become conscious of our national life and to rejoice in it, to recall what our country has done for each of us, and to ask ouselves what we can do for our country. —Oliver Wendell Holmes

America

Homer E. Dixon

I have followed your beautiful valleys
Dug out by the hand of God.
I have roamed your level prairies
Where herds of bison trod;
And I have climbed your rugged mountains,
Majestic, stern, and still,
And perched aloft on a lonesome crag
Where the winter's wind blew chill.

I have sat on the edge of the canyon's rim
And heard its waterfalls roar
And seen through the haze of mountain maze
The lonesome eagle soar.
On oceans deep where wild winds sweep
And waves roll loud and high,
I have wondered how God made it all
And the beautiful starlit sky.

O America, I love you
Deep as your mountains are high;
And my love for you will always be
True blue as your summer sky.
You are beautiful and noble,
Immense, rugged, and grand.
America, I love you,
My own, my native land.

This front porch in Beaufort, South Carolina, is decorated to celebrate the Fourth of July. Photograph by Dianne Dietrich Leis/Dietrich Leis Stock Photography.

The two most
important things
we can give our
children are roots
as deep as a
giant oak's and
wings as strong as
an eagle's.

—Jerry Apps

The Eagle

Alfred, Lord Tennyson

He clasps the crag with crooked hands;
Close to the sun in lonely lands,
Ringed with the azure world, he stands.
The wrinkled sea beneath him crawls;
He watches from his mountain walls
And like a thunderbolt he falls.

Eagles' Wings

Carolyn Elizabeth Grygiel

Today my heart wore eagles' wings
And I soared above the clouds;
High above these earthly shrouds
I sang the song of kings.

I found my gold in snow-crowned peaks
And glistening valleys far below,
Finding thereby all I seek
And ever need to know.

For after seeing starlight cry,
For after being kissed by rain,
For having soared beyond the sky,
I cannot be the same.

Today my heart wore eagles' wings,
Dare ask me have I changed!

The Symbol

Author Unknown

All through the ages—to this day
A symbol—reigns the bird of prey.
On nations' banners, forts, and gates,
Armor, currency, and estates;
Hovering there in bold contour,
A sign of strength in peace or war;
O'er lowest sect to station regal,
With stately mien, guards the eagle.

Pink twilight clouds hover over the rolling hills and flowering meadows of Zumwalt Prairie, rimmed by the Findley Buttes in Wallowa County, Oregon. Photograph by Terry Donnelly/Donnelly Austin Photography.

The Statue
of Liberty

Frank H. Keith

The torch of tolerance and light
Is in my tireless hand—
I send the flame of faith and truth
Across a blessed land.

One Nation

Clay Harrison

There is a joy in knowing
You are a part of something great,
A fellowship of brotherhood
That is found in every state.
We celebrate our differences
Throughout the tender years
That forged one nation under God
With blood and sweat and tears.

We are proud and independent,
A leader of the world.
We cherish evey freeedom
Where Old Glory is unfurled.
We wave our flags and celebrate
With fireworks and with tears
And know that every child can grow
To live free and have no fears.

Patriot

Shirley Sallay

Whenever I see Old Glory,
It gives a lift to my heart,
And the strains of the national anthem
Still make a teardrop start.
I love the excitement of a parade
And the uniformed men going by;
I am proud of my independence
On each new Fourth of July.
What a wonderful heritage America gives
To those who serve her true,
A haven for the troubled
And a home where respect is due.

*The magnificent Punch Bowl Falls in the Eagle Creek
Wilderness Area of Oregon's Columbia River Gorge is one of the most
popular scenic spots in the state. Photograph by Dennis Frates.*

Let Me Be Free

Vera Baisel

I heard the whistle of a train
As it sped swiftly on its way;
And as it ever fainter grew
I fancied I could hear it say,

"Come fly with me to worlds afar:
Away from all the noise and rush—
Where there is time to rest awhile
And hear the singing of a thrush;

"Where you can lie on cool, green grass
And gaze up in the azure sky,

While being fanned by dancing leaves,
As soft, white clouds go drifting by.

"Come stroll beside a rippling stream
From whence pure, sparkling water flows;
Sit down beneath a willow tree;
Forget the world with all its woes."

A slave to turmoil, stress, and strife
God never meant for man to be;
He made the woodlands and the plains
So that man's spirit could be free!

The shallow . . . consider liberty a release from all law,

from every constraint. The wise see in it, on the contrary, the potent Law of Laws,

namely, the fusion and combination of the conscious will, or partial individual law,

with those universal, eternal, unconscious ones, which run through all Time,

pervade history, prove immortality, give moral purpose to the

entire objective world, and the last dignity to human life. —WALT WHITMAN

Wildflowers crowd a stream in Banff National Park in Alberta, Canada.
Photograph by Christopher Talbot Frank.

The World We Make
Alfred Grant Walton

We make the world in which we live
By what we gather and what we give,
By our daily deeds and the things we say,
By what we keep or we cast away.

We make our world by the beauty we see
In a skylark's song or a lilac tree,
In a butterfly's wing, in the pale moon's rise,
And the wonder that lingers in midnight skies.

We make our world by the life we lead,
By the friends we have, by the books we read,
By the pity we show in the hour of care,
By the loads we lift and the love we share.

We make our world by the goals we pursue,
By the heights we seek and the higher view,
By hopes and dreams that reach the sun
And a will to fight till the heights are won.

Look to This Day!
Kalidasa

Look to this day!
For it is life, the very life of life.
In its brief course
Lie all the verities and realities of your existence:
    The bliss of growth;
    The glory of action;
    The splendor of achievement;
For yesterday is but a dream,
And tomorrow is only a vision;
But today, well lived, makes every yesterday
    a dream of happiness
And every tomorrow a vision of hope.
Look well, therefore, to this day!

The invitation to romp on the beach is irresistible on Nantucket island, Massachusetts. Photograph by William H. Johnson.

READERS' FORUM

Snapshots from our IDEALS readers

Left: "Listen to me play," three-year-old Olivia Grace Sherlock seems to be saying. Her grandmother, Monica Sherlock, of Bedford, Virginia, is a piano instructor and looks forward to giving lessons to Olivia Grace and her sister, Emily. Tom Sherlock, the proud grandfather, and parents, Tom and Melissa Sherlock, are all awaiting the first recital.

Below left: Just perfect! Bonnie Kate Hester, two-and-a-half years old, is the daughter of Tim and Virginia Hester of Georgia. When she visits her grandparents, James and Louise Hester of Benoit, Mississippi, her favorite place to sit is in this tiny chair.

Below right: "So many toys and not enough time." Seven-month-old Sophia Marie Biehler, daughter of Grant and Melinda Biehler of Tualatin, Oregon, enjoys all of her bright playthings.

Top right: Ballet beauty doubled—Lauren and Lindey English of Sammamish, Washington, are the five-year-old nieces of Naomi Boyce of Bonner Springs, Kansas, and the granddaughters of Virginia English.

Right: Eighteen-month-old Sean Siddens, son of Patrick and Jill Siddens of Owassa, Michigan, and great-grandson of Keith and Lettie Siddens, of Albany, New York, is the best-looking flower in the garden.

THANK YOU for sharing your family snapshots with *IDEALS*. We hope to hear from other readers who would like to share theirs with the *IDEALS* family. Please include a self-addressed, stamped envelope if you would like the snapshots returned; or keep your originals for safekeeping and send duplicates, along with your name, address, and telephone number to:

Readers' Forum
Ideals Publications
535 Metroplex Drive, Suite 250
Nashville, Tennessee 37211

Dear Reader,

The summers of my childhood were defined by days of playing at creekside with my best friends who lived only a few houses down the street, but summer can also evoke memories more serious.

The small community where I live sponsors a town picnic and an evening concert on the Fourth of July. While the orchestra plays music of the 1940s and folks of all ages laugh and clap as the children eat the last of the watermelons, I will pause to reflect on the reason for this holiday. Although Independence day is often taken for granted and simply marks the midpoint of the summer, as the daughter of a veteran of two wars, I can never hear the national anthem without feeling proud.

I hope your summer has many long, sunny afternoons and your backyard stays crowded with family and neighbors, a few barking dogs, and cool crocks filled with homemade peach ice cream.

Marjorie L. Lloyd

ideals

Publisher, Patricia A. Pingry
Editor, Marjorie Lloyd
Designer, Marisa Calvin
Copy Editor, Marie Brown
Permissions Editor, Patsy Jay
Contributing Writers, Maud Dawson, Joan Donaldson, Pamela Kennedy, Melissa Lester, D. Fran Morley, Patsy Pittman

ACKNOWLEDGMENTS

BUTLER, EDITH SHAW. "The Meadow Lark" from *The American Agriculturist.* Submitted by Edith Shaw Butler with the permission of the publisher. DICKINSON, EMILY "Two Butterflies" from *The Poems of Emily Dickinson,* edited by Ralph W. Franklin, Cambridge, Mass,: The Belknap Press of Harvard University Press, Copyright © 1951, 1955, 1979, 1983 1998 by the President and Fellows of Harvard College. Reprinted by permission of the publishers and the Trustees of Amherst College. JAQUES, EDNA. "Home Relish" from *The Golden Road.* by Edna Jaques. Copyright © 1953 by Thomas Allen Ltd. Used by permission of Louise Bonnell.
Our sincere thanks to the following authors, some of whom we were unable to locate: May Allread Baker for "Summer Pastorale" from *The Cincinnati Enquirer;* Marel Brown for "Noon," originally published in *Red Hills* by Broadman Press; Martha Haskell Clark for "Red Geraniums" from *Best Loved Poems of the American People,* 1936; Frances Frost for "Father" from *Favorite Poems Old and New,* Doubleday, 1957; Frank H. Keith for "The Statue of Liberty" from *The Naperville Sun,* 1972; Eiluned Lewis for "Country Born" from *Favorite Poems Old and New,* Doubleday, 1957; Henry Polk Lowenstein for "To the Skylark" from the *Davis Anthology of Newspaper Verse for 1927;* Margaret Neel for "Alfalfa" from *The Denver Post,* 1964; Mary Newlin Roberts for "His Hand" from the *Ladies Home Journal,* 1940s; Daisy Covin Walker for "Things I Love" from the *Davis Anthology of Newspaper Verse for 1938;* Alfred Grant Walton for "The World We Make" from *Highways to Happiness,* 1938. We also thank those those authors, or their heirs, some of whom we were unable to locate, who submitted original poems or articles to *Ideals* for publication. Every possible effort has been made to acknowledge ownership of material used.

*Right:*Number One! Joseph Keith Ahlstrom is the first great-grandchild of IDEALS reader Mary Curtis of Caledonia, Illinois. Parents Keith and Lisa Ahlstrom make their home in San Diego, California.